Get Your Poop in a Group

Written & Illustrated by B. K. Hixson

Get Your Poop in a Group

Copyright © 2003
First Printing • February 2003
B. K. Hixson

Published by Loose in the Lab, Inc.
9462 South 560 West
Sandy, Utah 84070

www.looseinthelab.com

Library of Congress Cataloging-in-Publication Data:

Hixson, B. K.
    Get Your Poop in a Group/B. K. Hixson
    p.   cm.-(Loose in the Lab Science Series)

    Includes index
    ISBN 0-931801-01-0
  1. Scientific Data Collection and Graphing—juvenile literature. [1. Graphing 2. Experiments] I. B. K. Hixson II. Loose in the Lab III. Title IV. Series
QP441.D54   2003
152.14

Printed in the United States of America

Dedication

E. V. Evans

My father-in-law, pictured here during his junior high school Halloween party, dressed up in a US Navy uniform, pretending to have just endured the longest ship-to-shore battle in US Naval history, courtesy of a little spat between Dwight D. Eisenhower and the Government of North Korea. This proves once again that those boys from Idaho will go to almost any lengths to get a cold beer—hopping a boat to Asia notwithstanding.

All that aside, more than one person has heard Shaun Davis claim that the greatest compliment bestowed upon a person would be to name a performing arts arena at a major American university in their honor. Harney, of course just to be contrary, would snap his suspenders and note that being inducted into the Pro Rodeo Hall of Fame would trump the arena thing any day of the week. And, not to be outdone, Ted would always boast that his brother was the WHO of the Who's Who of Cardiology Miracles in the Magic Valley. Well, all of that discussion can be put to rest now. War medals, arenas, and gold belt buckles are all darned impressive but, honestly, to have a book dedicated to you extolling your lifelong advice to anyone in earshot—"Get Your Poop in a Group"—well, let me say it for you ... "There just aren't enough words."

Many Happy Trails!

P.S. Pass me another cold one.

Acknowledgments

I should really thank Henry Dietz for being a coward, Rudy Rojas for being woefully unprepared, and Charlie Kingston for being desperate. Collectively and in order, they were my department chairman, supervising administrator, and first principal. When I was hired to teach 7th grade physical science at Fowler Junior High two days before school started, I was unknowingly thrust into the oncoming headlamps of the impromptu curriculum development train. Little did I know that writing and creating lesson plans and cartoon characters out of sheer desperation would turn into a full-time occupation that took me all over the United States. So, whatever shortcomings you three gentlemen had as mentors in the field of science education, you more than made up for it by leaving me to invent my own brand of science teaching. Thanks for your lack of direction. Sincerely.

As for my educational outlook, the hands-on perspective, and the use of humor in the classroom, Dr. Fox, my senior professor at Oregon State University, gets the credit for shaping my educational philosophy while simultaneously recognizing that even at the collegiate level we were on to something a little different. He did his very best to encourage, nurture, and support me while I was getting basketloads of opposition for being willing to swim upstream. There were also several colleagues who helped to channel my enthusiasm during those early, formative years of teaching: Dick Bishop, Dick Hinton, Dee Strange, Connie Ridgway, and Linda Zimmermann. Thanks for your patience, friendship, and support.

Next up are all the folks who get to do the dirty work that makes the final publication look so polished but very rarely get the credit they deserve. Our resident graphics guru, Kris Barton, gets a nod for scanning and cleaning the artwork you find on these pages, as well as putting together the graphics that make up the cover. A warm Yankee yahoo to Eve Laubner, our editor, who passes her comments on so that Kathleen Hixson and Eve Laubner (once again) can take turns simultaneously proofreading the text while mocking my writing skills.

Once we have a finished product, it is placed in the capable hands of Gary Facente, Selina Gerow, Louisa Walker, Tracy St. Pierre, and the Delta Education gang so they can market and ship the books, collect the money, and send us a couple of nickels. It's a short thank-you for some very important jobs.

Mom and Dad, as always, get the end credits. Thanks for the education, encouragement, and love. And for Kathy and the kids—Porter, Shelby, Courtney, and Aubrey—hugs and kisses, forever and ever.

Repro Rights

There is very little about this book that is truly formal, but at the insistence of our wise and esteemed counsel, let us declare: *No part of this book may be reproduced or utilized in any form or by any means, electronic or mechanical, including photocopying, recording, or by any information storage and retrieval system, without permission in writing from the publisher.* That would be us.

More Legal Stuff
Official disclaimer for you aspiring scientists and lab groupies. This is a hands-on science book. By the very intent of the design, you will be directed to use common, nontoxic, household items in a safe and responsible manner to avoid injury to yourself and others who are present while you are pursuing your quest for knowledge and enlightenment in the world of science. Just make sure that you have a fire blanket handy and a wall-mounted video camera to corroborate your story.

If, for some reason, perhaps even beyond your own control, you have an affinity for disaster, we wish you well. *But we in no way take any responsibility for any injury that is incurred to any person using the information provided in this book or for any damage to personal property or effects that is directly or indirectly a result of the suggested activities contained herein.* Translation: You're on your own, despite the fact that many have preceded you in the lab. Take heed and follow directions. Never perform a lab without clean underwear on, just in case you have to go to the Emergency Room. And please, don't put anything up your nose bigger than a roll of quarters.

Less Formal Legal Stuff
If you happen to be a home schooler or very enthusiastic school teacher, please feel free to make copies of this book for your classroom or personal family use—one copy per student, up to 35 students. If you would like to use an experiment from this book for a presentation to your faculty or school district, we would be happy to oblige. Just give us a whistle and we will send you a release for the particular lab activity you wish to use. Please contact us at the address below. Thanks.

Special Requests
Loose in the Lab, Inc.
9462 South 560 West
Sandy, Utah 84070

© 2003 • B. K. Hixson • Loose in the Lab

Table of Contents

Dedication	3
Acknowledgments	4
Repro Rights	5
Lab Safety	8
Recommended Materials Suppliers	11

The National Content Standards (Grades 1-4)
Use data to construct a reasonable explanation. This aspect of the standard emphasizes the students' thinking as they use data to formulate explanations. Even at the earliest grade levels, students should learn what constitutes evidence and judge the merits or strength of the data and information that will be used to make explanations. After students propose an explanation, they will appeal to the knowledge and evidence they obtained to support their explanations. Students should check their explanations against scientific knowledge, experiences, and observations of others.

The National Content Standards (Grades 5-8)
Use appropriate tools and techniques to gather, analyze, and interpret data. The use of tools and techniques, including mathematics, will be guided by the question asked and the investigations students design. The use of computers for collection, summary, and display of evidence is part of this standard. Students should be able to access, gather, store, retrieve, and organize data, using hardware and software designed for these purposes.

Develop descriptions, explanations, predictions, and models using evidence. Students should base their explanation on what they observed, and as they develop cognitive skills, they should be able to differentiate explanation from description—providing causes for effects and establishing relationships based on evidence and logical argument. This standard requires a subject matter knowledge base so the students can effectively conduct investigations, because developing explanations establishes connections between the content of science and the contexts within which students develop new knowledge.

The Big Ideas About Data, Data Tables, & Graphing

1. Data is information. It can take the form of physical measurements, written observations, drawings, chemical changes, impressions, collections, photographs, digital images, or sound recordings.

> *Lab #1: Portable Pan Flutes (measurements)*   18
> *Lab #2: Optical Illusion Gallery (opinions)*   22
> *Lab #3: BBQ Sponge Gardens (drawings)*   30
> *Lab #4: Black Ink, You Think? (chemical changes)*   34
> *Lab #5: Fossil Fish Diggings (impressions & collections)*   40

2. Data tables are used to organize the measurements and observations collected while conducting scientific research. Data tables have titles that describe the data. They also list the constants and variables tested as well as the units used to measure them.

> *Lab #6: Heads or Tails (tabulation data tables)*   46
> *Lab #7: Nail Magnets (single variable data tables)*   52
> *Lab #8: Pendulum Puzzles (constants)*   56
> *Lab #9: Calculated Leverage (multiple variables)*   59

3. Once the data has been organized and recorded into a data table, a picture of that data can be constructed using pictographs, pie graphs, bar graphs, line graphs, or best fit graphs.

> *Lab #10: Stacking Water (pictographs)*   72
> *Lab #11: Conductivity Tester (pie graphs)*   77
> *Lab #12: Liquid Densities (bar graphs)*   81
> *Lab #13: Instant Hand Warmer (line graphs)*   86
> *Lab #14: Heli Data (best fit graphs)*   90

Glossary   96
Index   102

Lab Safety

Contained herein are 14 science activities to help you better understand the value of careful data collection and display. However, since you are on your own in this journey, we thought it prudent to share some basic wisdom and experience in the safety department.

Read the Instructions

An interesting concept, especially if you are a teenager. Take a minute before you jump in and get going to read all of the instructions as well as warnings. If you do not understand something, stop and ask an adult for help.

Clean Up All Messes

Keep your lab area clean. It will make it easier to put everything away at the end and may also prevent contamination and the subsequent germination of a species of mutant tomato bug larva. You will also find that chemicals perform with more predictability if they are not poisoned with foreign molecules.

Organize

Translation: Put it back where you get it. If you need any more clarification, there is an opening at the landfill for you.

Dispose of Poisons Properly

This will not be much of a problem with the labs that are suggested in this book. However, if you happen to wander over into one of the many disciplines that incorporates the use of more advanced chemicals, then we would suggest that you use great caution with the materials and definitely dispose of any and all poisons properly.

Practice Good Fire Safety

If there is a fire in the room, notify an adult immediately. If an adult is not in the room and the fire is manageable, smother the outbreak with a fire blanket or use a fire extinguisher. When the fire is contained, immediately send someone to find an adult. If, for any reason, you happen to catch on fire, **REMEMBER: Stop, Drop, and Roll.** Never run; it adds oxygen to the fire, making it burn faster, and it also scares the bat guano out of the neighbors when they see the neighbor kids running down the block doing an imitation of a campfire marshmallow without the stick.

Protect Your Skin

It is a good idea to always wear protective gloves whenever you are working with chemicals. Again, this particular book does not suggest or incorporate hazardous chemicals in its lab activities. But if you do happen to spill a chemical onto your skin, notify an adult immediately and then flush the area with water for 15 minutes. If irritation develops, have your parent or another responsible adult look at it. If it appears to be of concern, contact a physician. Take any information that you have about the chemical with you.

Lab Safety

Save Your Nose Hairs
Sounds like a cause celebre L.A. style, but it is really good advice. To smell a chemical to identify it, hold the open container six to ten inches down and away from your nose. Make a clockwise circular motion with your hand over the opening of the container, "wafting" some of the fumes toward your nose. This will allow you to safely smell some of the fumes without exposing yourself to a large dose of anything noxious. This technique may help prevent a nosebleed or your lungs from accidentally getting burned.

Wear Goggles If Appropriate
If the lab asks you to heat or mix chemicals, be sure to wear protective eyewear. Also have an eyewash station or running water available. You never know when something is going to splatter, splash, or react unexpectedly. It is better to look like a nerd and be prepared than schedule a trip down to pick out a Seeing Eye dog. If you do happen to accidentally get chemicals in your eye, flush the area for 15 minutes. If any irritation or pain develops, immediately go see a doctor.

Lose the Comedy Routine
You should have plenty of time scheduled during your day to mess around, but science lab is not one of them. Horseplay breaks glassware, spills chemicals, and creates unnecessary messes— things that parents do not appreciate. Trust us on this one.

No Eating
Do not eat while performing a lab. Putting your food in the lab area contaminates your food and the experiment. This makes for bad science and worse indigestion. Avoid poisoning yourself and goobering up your labware by observing this rule.

Happy and safe experimenting!

Recommended Materials Suppliers

For every lesson in this book, we offer a list of materials. Many of these are very easy to acquire, and if you do not have them in your home already, you will be able to find them at the local grocery or hardware store. For more difficult items, we have selected, for your convenience, a small but respectable list of suppliers who will meet your needs in a timely and economical manner. Call for a catalog or quote on the item that you are looking for, and they will be happy to give you a hand.

Loose in the Lab
9462 South 560 West
Sandy, UT 84070
Phone 1-888-403-1189
Fax 1-801-568-9586
www.looseinthelab.com

Nasco
901 Jonesville Ave.
Fort Atkinson, WI 53538
Phone 1-414-563-2446
Fax 1-920-563-8296
www.nascofa.com

Educational Innovations
151 River Rd.
Cos Cob, CT 06807
Phone 1-888-912-7474
Fax 1-203-629-2739
www.teachersource.com

Fisher Scientific
485 S. Frontage Rd.
Burr Ridge, IL 60521
Phone 1-800-955-1177
Fax 1-800-955-0740
www.fisheredu.com

Delta Education
80 NW Blvd.
Nashua, NH 03063
Phone 1-800-442-5444
Fax 1-800-282-9560
www.delta-education.com

Ward's Scientific
5100 W. Henrietta Rd.
Rochester, NY 14692
Phone 1-800-387-7822
Fax 1-716-334-6174
www.wardsci.com

Frey Scientific
100 Paragon Pkwy.
Mansfield, OH 44903
Phone 1-800-225-FREY
Fax 1-419-589-1546
www.freyscientific.com

Flinn Scientific
PO Box 219
Batavia, IL 60510
Phone 1-800-452-1261
Fax 1-630-879-6962
www.flinnsci.com

The Ideas, Lab Activities, & Applications

Graphing, Schmaphing

What's the Big Deal?

Oh, nothing really. Graphing just makes life easier and decision-making a little quicker. There are basically two reasons that you should not only learn how to construct data tables and use graphs but also incorporate them into your study of science: The reasons are organization and interpretation.

1. Organization

As a scientist, athlete, aspiring weather forecaster, doctor, mechanic, or whatever you decide to be, you are more than likely to be swamped with data. How much force was applied, how many free throws is she making, what is the current barometric pressure, how high is the cholesterol count, or what is the pulling capacity of the motor in torque pound feet? These are all questions that require data to be provided.

A little bit of data is fine, but what happens if you request or collect data for several weeks or years? You are in for a numerical brain cramp that will cause your upper lip to involuntarily curl and your eyebrows to spontaneously fuse. To avert this social faux pas and impending neolithic disaster, you are going to need a way to organize the information. That's where data tables and graphs come in.

Data tables and graphs give you a structure, like see-through cabinets, in which to store and organize your data so that you can find it easily and refer to it quickly. Once data is organized, then it is right there when you need to answer a question, prove a point, or double check a fact. This is the first step in being able to use data correctly.

... an Introduction

2. Interpretation

This is one of the main reasons that we collect and graph data. Numbers are nice because they are exact and informative, but if you need to make a quick decision, plotting all of those individual numbers into a single, quick-to-review picture allows you to interpret the data with ease. This helps you make decisions quickly and with confidence.

For example, everyone has seen those made-for-television hospital shows. Inevitably, they show a scene in a room where a patient is hooked to a life support monitor that tracks heartbeats. This monitor is constantly collecting, storing, organizing, and presenting this data as a line graph. The doctor can look at the line and instantly interpret the pile of data points and make a decision without having to look at each data point (single heartbeat) individually.

A lot of times, folks look at data tables and graphs not because they are trying to save someone's life but because they are making decisions about which product sells well for their company, how efficient a new airplane wing design appears to be, or whether or not the number of dogs loose in the neighborhood explains the sudden upswing in puppy chow sales. The point is that a graph is a picture of the data that has been collected. It allows you to quickly and efficiently analyze your data and, if necessary, draw a conclusion that you can act on.

Now you know why it helps to build data tables and draw graphs. This explians the importance of graphing. (Nobody really knows what "schmaphing" is anyway.)

Big Idea 1

Data is information. It can take the form of physical measurements, written observations, drawings, chemical changes, impressions, collections, photographs, digital images, or sound recordings.

Physical Measurements

What Do They Look Like?

Numbers. Lots of numbers. We start with this category because scientists most commonly collect and represent data using numbers. This is the kind of data that you will be looking to chase down most of the time. Whole numbers, numbers followed by decimals, positive numbers and negative numbers, lots of numbers with units behind them... all these types of numbers provide us with important information.

What Do They Tell Me?

Physical measurements tell you all kinds of things, such as how hot it is, how cold it might get, the amount of force needed to move an object, and how tall the bean plants have grown since Jack planted them two days ago. These types of things all provide *quantitative information*, which gives you specific details in the form of numbers. Another way of thinking of physical measurements is that they tell you how much of something there is—how much it weighs, measures, heats up, how much space it occupies, how fast it is traveling, or which note was produced when it squealed.

How Do I Collect This Data?

You always must collect measurements using the appropriate *instrument*. If you are collecting weather data, you will want to use thermometers, anemometers, barometers, or hygrometers. If you are measuring mass, you may use a spring balance, triple beam balance, simple pan balance, or atomic scale. Length is measured using rulers marked in either English or metric units, or both. Volume is collected using beakers, flasks, graduated cylinders, and pipettes, which give measurements in metric or English units.

To get started, you are going to learn how to turn an ordinary drinking straw into a flute that makes noise. Then you are going to tune your flute to a piano. Finally, after you get the note resonating out of your flute to match the vibrations of a single piano note, you will measure the flute and determine its length in centimeters. This is a piece of data for those paying attention to the proceedings.

Portable Pan Flutes

The Experiment
You will need a naked straw for this experiment. Once in the buff, the straw is cut following the pattern on the bottom of this page and flattened using the edge of a pair of scissors. Place the straw inside your mouth, just behind your lips, so that the ends are free to vibrate. When a large volume of air is pushed through the straw rapidly, it causes the cut plastic to vibrate, producing an obnoxious buzzing sound. Science for the auditorially tolerant.

Materials
5 Straws
1 Pair of scissors
1 Pair of lungs
1 Piano
1 Metric ruler, 30 cm

Procedure
1. We are going to start with the end of the straw. Place it on the table and flatten the ends with the blunt side of the scissor blade. Then, cut the top of the straw into the shape that is pictured at the right. Snip two small triangles from the end of the straw to produce the shape that you see here.

2. Once it is cut, flatten the end with a pair of scissors again. If it is a plastic straw (as opposed to paper), it may take several good hard rubs to get it flat.

3. Wet the cut end of the straw with your mouth. With the straw past your lips an inch or so, blow as hard as you can. The cut ends should vibrate and produce an obnoxious sound. If you have a difficult time doing this, it may be because you are not using enough air or because you need to put more of the straw in your mouth. Blow from your diaphragm (stomach area) and really push.

4. Once you have the straw flute down pat, take the scissors and, while you are blowing into the straw, cut the straw shorter and shorter, changing the pitch of the straw with each snip.

5. Now comes the tricky part. Make another long, straw flute. Using a piano as a point of reference, blow into the straw and find the matching note on the piano. This is Note Number 1. Measure the length of the straw in cm and record that length in the data table on the next page.

6. Now you are going to reverse the process. Press the piano key that is two white keys to the right of the first key you pressed. Using the scissors, cut another straw flute, play it, and slowly shorten the length until you find that the note you play matches the note that was just played on the piano. Measure the length of this straw and enter it into the data table.

7. Repeat this process, pressing keys for notes on the piano that are five and seven white keys to the right of the original one. Play, cut, and measure the lengths of the straws that produce the two matching notes. Then enter the data into your data table.

Portable Pan Flutes

How Come, Huh?

As the air passes over the opening that has been cut, it causes the cut ends of the straw to vibrate. The movement of the plastic compresses the air inside the tube, creating sound waves which come out the other end of the straw. The pitch of the instrument is directly proportional to the length. The longer the instrument, the lower the pitch and vice-versa.

Collecting the Data

When you are collecting physical measurements, you will probably be putting them into a data table much like the one that you see below.

Be sure that you add a title to your data table. Pick a title that is descriptive and tells you what you are collecting. Capitalize the first letter of each word. You will also want to make columns and list the constant (the note in this case) and the variable (the length of the straw). Include the units that you are measuring the variables in. Here's an example of how you would create a data table for this lab:

Variable Length Straw Flutes

Note	Length of Straw (cm)
1	
2	
3	
4	

Opinions

What Do They Look Like?
Opinion Tallies. Opinions, in the context of a scientific experiment, are usually solicited by the interviewer in the form of a question, such as "Do you like this smell, yes or no?", "Which line is longer, the top or the bottom?", or "Are you satisfied with your long-distance phone service?" The interviewer then puts a tally mark in the column that corresponds with the answer given.

What Do They Tell Me?
Opinion tallies usually give you an idea of **what people think** or, in the case of this lab, how they perceive an optical illusion.

How Do I Collect Opinion Data?
Figure out what you want to know and **start asking questions.** Make sure each question can be answered with one of two responses, like yes/no. People such as market researchers and psychologists sometimes structure questions that can be answered in many ways. This gives them a good understanding of how people think and of what opinion they have. However, we are not going to get into that. The opinions that you collect will be simple answers to simple questions.

Optical Illusion Gallery

The Experiment

This is a collection of optical illusions. As a general rule, these illusions work because, through experience, we develop ideas or notions about how our world should appear. When we see something new, we base our evaluation on what we already know.

Several of these illusions are based on classical line drawings that have been around for a long time and use the relationship between lines and space to create the illusion. Illusion 1 is the perfect example. Look at Illusion 1 and determine which line is the longest and which is the shortest. If you take a ruler and measure each of the lines, you may be surprised at what you find.

Illusions 2, 3, and 4 are also created by adding reference lines or objects that trick the eye into thinking that the distances are different. Again, a ruler will bring the truth to light.

The 5th illusion is simply a test of how you look at a picture. It was created by the cartoonist W.H. Breenan in 1915, and some psychologists will tell you that it provides insights into how you view the world. We just think it is a cool illustration when you finally see both images.

Procedure

Examine each of the displays on this page and the ones that follow. Try to answer each question based on what you see. After you find an answer, take a ruler and measure to see if your answer is correct or if the illusion has tricked your eyes.

The first question is below.

1. Look at the five lines below. Which line appears to be the shortest? ____

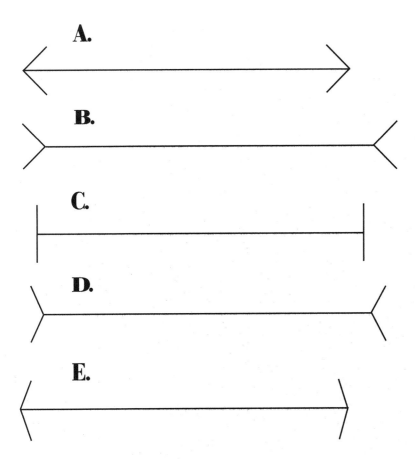

Optical Illusion Gallery

2. Below, is the letter B closer to letters A or C?

3. Which circle, A or B, is larger in diameter?

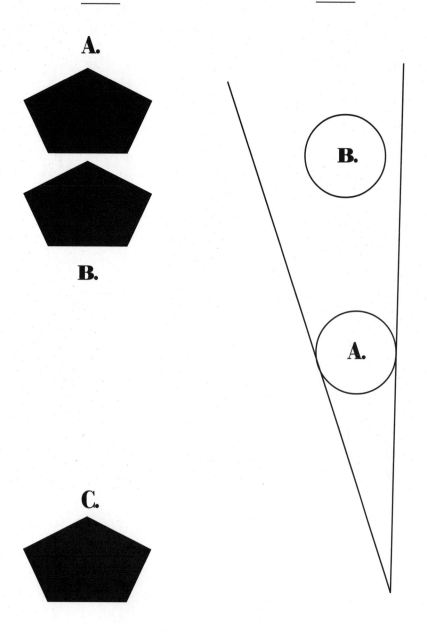

Get Your Poop in a Group • B. K. Hixson

4. Which circle, A or B, is larger in diameter?

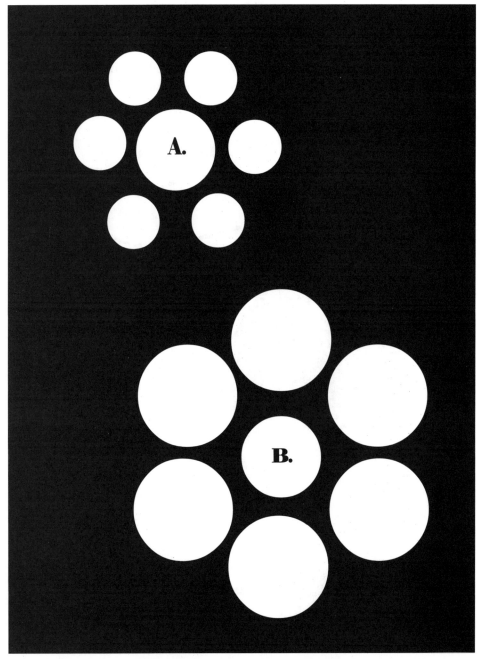

Optical Illusion Gallery

5. This illusion is guided by your initial perception of the image you see. When you look at the picture below, you will either see an old lady looking down and toward you or a young lady looking down and away.

Look at the illustration below and trace the outline of the old lady's nose with a red pencil. Outline the nose of the young lady with a green pencil.

Collecting the Data

When you are collecting opinions, you will probably be putting them into data tables much like the ones that you see below. For each piece of data you collect, you will want to make a tally mark to represent the answer that was given. A single tally mark looks like a simple "1". Every set of 5 tally marks is grouped together with the 5th mark placed on a diagonal. (⊬⊬⊬)

1. From page 23: Which line appears to be the shortest?

A	
B	
C	
D	
E	

2. From page 24: Is the letter B closer to letters A or C?

A	
C	

3. From page 24: Which circle, A or B, is larger in diameter?

A	
B	

4. From page 25: Which circle, A or B, is larger in diameter?

A	
B	

5. From page 26: Do you see an old lady or a young lady?

Old lady	
Young lady	

Drawings

What Do They Look Like?

They say that a picture is worth a thousand words, and if that is true, you can save a lot of paper when preparing your lab reports. Drawings, illustrations, murals, and schematic diagrams all allow scientists to communicate their observations and ideas quickly with **a picture**.

What Do They Tell Me?

For starters, a picture is an excellent way to **describe visually**, in a very small amount of space, **the appearance an object**. Field biologists, wildlife experts, botanists, anatomists, microbiologists, oceanographers, and countless others all use drawings to record the appearance of organisms (plants, animals, and microbes) that they are studying.

Drawings are not only used for animate objects (things that are alive) but they are also used to describe inanimate objects like rocks, land formations, clouds, and machines.

Drawings of both animate and inanimate objects can be used to **depict changes over time**. Animals and plants grow and go through cycles. Ecosystems with indigenous species of animals and plants can be depicted with drawings. The water, nitrogen, and carbon cycles can be described with a single picture as opposed to pages and pages full of words. The change in the position of the continents over time would be almost impossible to understand without an illustration created from books of data. The changes in landforms over the past hundred years can be seen by comparing the illustrations of early explorers with pictures of the same sites today. In all these examples, as well as many others, drawings make it easy to show and see changes over time.

Drawings can also be used to **instruct** other scientists in **how to replicate their work**. Diagrams of lab set-ups, electrical circuitry, machines, and techniques allow scientists to review, replicate, and authenticate one another's work. This is a very important part of science.

How Do I Make a Drawing?

Sharpen your pencil, get out your drawing pad, and have at it.

BBQ Sponge Gardens

The Experiment
This reaction produces crystals by evaporation. When the crystal-growing solution is poured on the briquette, sponge, old sock, rag, or whatever, the liquid is soaked up. The liquid then slowly evaporates into the air. As it evaporates, it leaves behind the salts that were originally dissolved in the solution. These salts remain as beautiful and, let us forewarn you, *extremely delicate* crystals.

An indicator of a chemical reaction is the production of a new compound. Here, salt, bluing, water, and ammonia are mixed together to produce a new, chemically distinct compound.

Materials
1   Charcoal briquette, piece of sponge, old sock, or rag
1   Pie tin
1   Bottle of crystal-growing solution
    or
    50 mL Table salt
    10 mL Ammonia
    100 mL Water
    50 mL Laundry bluing
    1 Quart jar
    1 Spoon
1   Hand lens
1   Pair of goggles

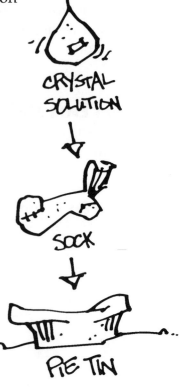

Procedure
1. If you are using ready-made crystal solution, skip this step. If you are making your own from scratch, mix the following in a large quart jar—100 mL water, 10 mL household ammonia, 50 mL laundry bluing, and 50 mL table salt. Stir with a spoon until all of the contents are thoroughly mixed.

2. Place the sponge or old sock in the pie tin and pour the entire bottle of crystal-growing solution over the briquette, sponge, sock, or rag. Add the solution until the liquid comes right up to the rim of the pie tin.

3. Place the pie tin in a warm, sunny location so that the solution will evaporate. The crystals will begin to appear in one to two hours and will continue to grow until all of the liquid has evaporated.

The sponge, sock, or other material will start to sport a collection of very delicate, powdery crystals that will collapse if you touch them or even breathe in their general direction—definitely no sneezing.

How Come, Huh?

All of the ingredients that you mixed together dissolved and went into solution. They are happy there but are subject to changes at the whim of the physical world. In this case, the liquids, water and ammonia, tend to evaporate if they are left out in the open air for a long time.

When the liquid evaporates from the pie tin, the heavier chemicals, the salts, are left behind. They try to go, migrating to the very top of the pile of matter that is in the tin, but when it comes right down to it, the liquid evaporates and the heavier chemicals are left behind. This is what produces the beautiful, fine crystals that you see in the tin. The more of the solution that evaporates, the bigger the crystals will grow, and this takes place until all of the liquid is gone.

BBQ Sponge Gardens

Collecting the Data

Drawings give you the opportunity to use a single picture that is more effective than several pages of words might be. Observe the crystals at the time intervals listed below and draw a picture of what they look like from a top view.

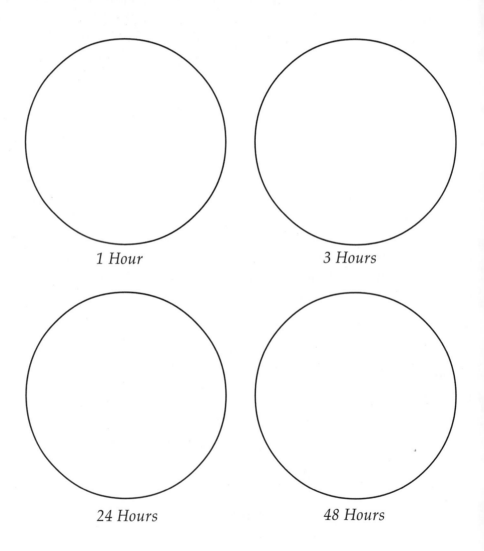

1 Hour

3 Hours

24 Hours

48 Hours

Chemical Changes

What Do They Look Like?

Chemical changes occur when a new compound is formed as a result of a reaction between two or more chemicals. It can be very subtle and undetectable to the naked eye, or very dramatic and impossible to ignore, like an explosion.

The kinds of chemical changes that we are interested in for this discussion come from a technique used in chemistry called chromatography. The word *chroma* means color, and we are guessing that you noticed the word *graph* within the larger word. Chromatography is the creation of a color graph that is made by separating chemicals that have been mixed into a group back out into individual bands or layers of distinct colors. The end product is a long, skinny piece of **paper that has bands of colors stretching from the bottom toward the top**.

What Do They Tell Me?

This rainbow of colors, called a chromatograph, **allows the scientist to separate the individual pigments or ink colors that are present in the sample**. In the case of black ink, it is all of the different colors that have been used to create the ink compound. In the case of a plant, it is the different pigments used by the plant to create the flower or build the leaf that collects sunlight.

How Do I Make a Chromatograph to Show Chemical Changes?

Funny you should ask. Turn the page.

Black Ink, You Think?

The Experiment

Black ink is not black. Silly as that may sound at first, it's true. Black inks have all sorts of colors hidden in them. Sometimes as many as six distinct colors can be separated out and identified.

One of the processes that allows you to separate out these colors is called chromatography. *Chroma* translates to color, and a *graph* is a picture. So chromatography is a color picture of the mixture of ink that you placed on the paper.

Materials

- 3 Toobes or large drinking glasses
- Water
- 1 Pair of scissors
- 3 Black, water-soluble, felt-tip pens
- 3 Craft sticks
- 3 Strips of absorbent paper, each $3/4$-inch wide by 12 inches long

Procedure

1. Add an inch of water to the bottom of a Toobe. A Toobe is a large acrylic cylinder that we use to conduct experiments. A large glass works just as well.

2. Cut three long, slender pieces of paper that are 3/4-inch wide and 12 inches long. Using a water-soluble, felt-tip pen, make a thick, black dot 1 inch up from the bottom of one of the strips of paper, as shown in the illustration on the next page.

3. Lower the paper so that it just touches the bottom of the Toobe, but make sure that the dot of black ink does not get into the water. If it looks like the dot is going to get wet, pull the paper out, empty out a bit of water, and lower the paper back into the Toobe.

Chromatograph

4. Place a craft stick on top of the Toobe and tape the paper to it so that it holds it in place. Your final set-up should look like the illustration below. Set the Toobe in an area where it will remain undisturbed.

Repeat this procedure two more times using the other pens, papers, and Toobes.

5. Make observations every hour for as long as possible. After 24 hours, your separation will be complete.

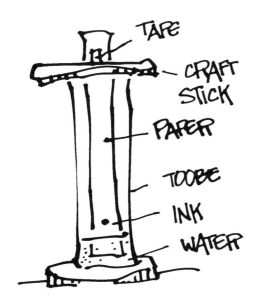

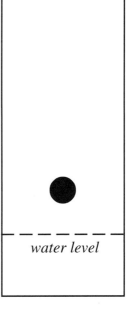

water level

6. When the chomatograph is complete, either cut your separation and tape it in the space provided at the right or, using colored pencils, copy the separations as accurately as you can.

Black Ink, You Think?

How Come, Huh?

The separation of pigments using this technique is called paper chromatography. As the water travels up the paper, it dissolves the ink, which is water-soluble, and literally picks it up, carrying the different colors with it. Every color migrates at different speeds and different distances. This is due to colors' differences in shapes and weights. As the water travels up the paper, the heavier inks get left behind and dry in place; the light, easier-to-transport inks zip along with the water.

When the chomatograph is done, you will see an outline of where the black dot used to be, along with several different colors, depending on the maker of the pen, separated into bands that migrated up the paper.

Collecting the Data

When the process is complete, you have three options. First, **tape the actual chromatographs into your lab report**. Nothing like the real thing when you are collecting and presenting data.

If there are several of you working together, the first option does not work for everyone, so whoever draws the short straw will get to measure the colors and **draw a replica of the actual chromatograph**.

The third option is a little pricey. Take the chromatographs down to a copy shop and **make color copies** to include in your reports.

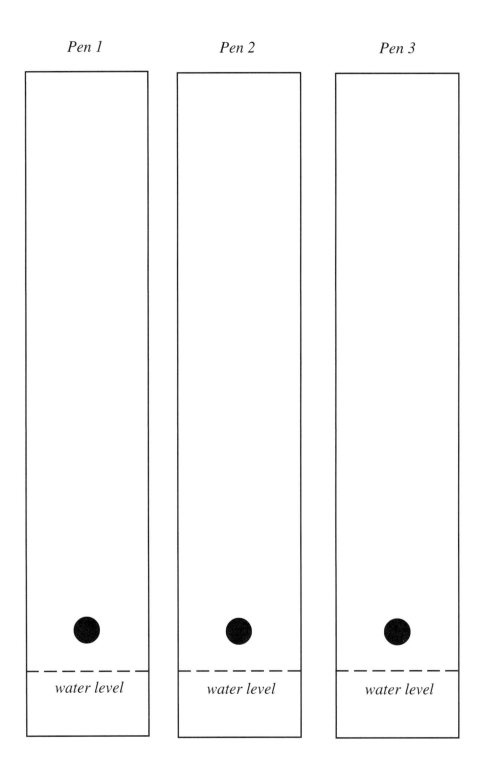

Casts, Collections, & Impressions

What Do They Look Like?

Collections are items that are stored in museums, universities, high schools, and even science laboratories. You can have collections of **rocks, pressed plants, stuffed animals, animals in jars, slides of samples of bacteria, metals, coins, paper,** you name it. If you can pick it up and store it in something, then you can make a collection of it.

Occasionally it is difficult or impossible to collect something and take it with you. Indian petroglyphs come to mind. A petroglyph is an ancient picture, sometimes thousands of years old, that was etched into the surface of a stone wall. These etchings can be found on the sides of many canyons, so, in addition to the fact that the local tribes would be quite ticked if you carted their wall art off to store at your school, it would be almost impossible.

Other times, fossils are embedded into rock that cannot be removed conveniently or without great expense. In those cases, you can take an impression by creating a **rubbing** or possibly a **plaster cast** of the actual item. By doing this, you can leave the item where you found it and still collect the data that you need.

What Do They Tell Me?

Collections allow other scientists to **examine the specimens firsthand**. This is particularly helpful if the collection comes from a place that is far away. The collection, rubbing, or cast allows the scientist to examine the objects without having the expense of traveling halfway around the world.

How Do I Make One?

To start a **collection,** all you have to do is bend over and **pick up an item of interest**. Preserve and label it. The label should include the common name of the item collected, the scientific name, and the date and location of the collecting site. You will also want to include the name of the collector (you) and any other relevant information.

A **rubbing** is done by putting a piece of paper over the object that you wish to collect and gently **rubbing the surface of the paper with a fat piece of crayon.** (Using the length of a crayon that has had its paper wrapper peeled off will make the job easy.) As the crayon crosses the irregular surface of the fossil, colored crayon wax is left on the paper. This crayon wax outlines the fossil.

Finally, a **plaster cast** can be made by **pushing the fossil into a piece of clay and then taking a mold of the impression in the clay.** You will collect specimens in all of these ways in the next lab activity.

Fossil Fish Diggings

The Experiment

Fossils are found in a number of different forms. They can take the form of impressions, casts, mineral replacements, objects embalmed in amber, and sometimes objects that have been buried in sediment.

The fossil fish specimen that you are going to use in this experiment is one of the last type. The fish died, it fell to the bottom of the lake, it was buried in mud before it could rot or be cannibalized by other fish, and 50 million years later it reappears at the end of a hammer and chisel.

You are going to use this fish to practice labeling a collected specimen, take a rubbing of it, and also create a plaster replica.

Materials

- 1 Fish fossil
- 1 Lump of clay, 4 oz.
- 1 Wax cup, 5 oz.
- 1 Craft stick
- 1 Strip of cardboard, 1 inch by 8 inches
- 1 Baggie of plaster of Paris, 4 oz.
- 1 Crayon or pencil
  Water

Procedure

1. Make a label for your specimen, as if you had collected it in the field. Read the paragraph on the next page and create a label from a separate sheet of paper using the pattern provided.

2. The fossil fish that you have is the great granddaddy to the modern day herring. It stands to reason that the common name of this fish is herring. It was found near Kemmerer, Wyoming, 50 million years ago in an Eocene Age formation called the Green River Formation. The scientific name is <u>Knightia</u> <u>sp</u>. It was collected, at least by you, on the date that you are completing this lab.

_____

Common Name

_____

Scientific Name

Formation:_____

Collected in:_____

Collected by:_____

Date:_____ Specimen #: _____

When you are finished with your label, place it in a collecting box with your specimen. This way, your fossil is identified, you know where it is, and it will be easy to pull it out and reference it. Your data is safe for the long haul. On to rubbings and molds.

Fossil Fish Diggings

3. Making a rubbing is relatively easy. Place the fossil on a hard, flat surface. Place a piece of paper over the fossil. Using a crayon that has been denuded of its wrapper, rub the edge of the crayon over the surface of the paper.

As the crayon hits the bumps and ridges created by the bones in the fish, crayon wax will be deposited more in some places than in others, and this will create an impression of the fish on the paper. Try it in the space below.

4. Now with labeling and rubbings behind us, casts are the only things left to go. Take the clay and mold it into a pancake shape that is 4 inches in diameter and roughly 3/4-inch thick.

5. Holding the fish fossil upside down, push it into the clay, making a reverse impression. Gently remove the fossil. Make as many impressions as you like. You've just created something called a mortality plate.

6. Roll the strip of cardboard into a loop and push it into the clay, forming a border around your best fossil impression. This will hold the plaster over the impressions in the clay. Use the illustration at the right as a guide.

7. Add the plaster of Paris to the wax cup. Slowly add water, stirring the mixture with the craft stick. When the plaster is the consistency of thick pudding, pour it into the impression. Fill the mold up to the level of the cardboard.

8. Set the fossil in a place where it will remain undisturbed for about a half hour. When the plaster is hard to the touch, gently peel the clay away from the bottom of the mold and remove the cardboard from the sides. What you have is a replica, or cast, of the original fossil. This kind of fossil is created when sediment fills the tracks or impressions left behind by animals or plants. The sediment hardens over time and produces a replica, or close copy.

9. Make a label similar to the label used for the real fossil. This will allow you to identify the cast.

Collecting the Data

The collections go in the box and on a shelf in a closet, the rubbings go in a notebook, and the casts are also placed in a labeled box to be stored for later use.

Big Idea 2

Data tables are used to organize the measurements and observations collected while conducting scientific research.

Types of Data Tables

What Do They Look Like?
There are basically three kinds of data tables.

    A. **Tabulation data tables** allow you to collect and organize large samples of data based on one or a couple of variables. Typically, the information you want to remember can be recorded in a column using tally marks. Tables are typically aligned in a horizontal plane. *Do the lab, Heads or Tails.*

    B. **Single variable data tables** are set up to record a single variable against a constant. These data tables have two columns, one for the variable and one for the constant. They can run either horizontally or vertically. *Do the lab, Nail Magnets.*

    C. **Multiple variable data tables** are set up to record several variables against a constant. These data tables have three or more columns for the variables and one for the constant. They run either horizontally or vertically and allow you to compare different conditions at the same time. *Do the lab, Calculated Leverage.*

What Do They Tell Me?
All data tables allow you the opportunity to record data in an organized manner. The information is recorded against a standard, such as time, temperature, or distance. The standard is called a constant. Because the data is recorded in an organized fashion, it is easy to locate and compare specific pieces of data.

How Do I Make Them?
That's why we have turned to this section.

Heads or Tails

The Experiment
When you flip a penny into the air a hundred times, probability tells us that it will most likely land heads up half the time and tails up half the time. When you spin a penny a hundred times, you get an entirely different result. What comes up more often, heads or tails, and why?

Fortunately, it's lab time and time for an introduction to tabulation data tables.

Materials
1   <u>New</u>, Lincoln head, penny
1   Hard surface
1   Pencil
    Very good record keeping

Procedure
1. Construct two tabulation data tables or use the examples that we provide for you on page 48.

2. Spin the penny on a hard surface. When the penny comes to rest, place a tally mark in the appropriate row, heads or tails, depending on how the penny landed.

3. Spin the penny 100 times. Continuing to use tally marks, record the number of heads and the number of tails that you get each time. Bundle your marks in groups of 5.

4. Now, flip the penny 100 times in the air and catch the coin each time. Record your observations in the second data table.

What Do Tabulation Data Tables Look Like?

They have a title, list two or more choices, and tally marks are used to record the results of the experiment or opinions of the survey. They are typically horizontal.

What Do They Tell Me?

Tabulation data tables are generally used to **record opinions or choices**. This kind of data table does not necessarily need a constant. It can be used to record such things as the favorite fruit, from a choice of 5, among a group of kids, the results of a coin toss over a sample of 100 tosses, or your friends' favorite movie from a choice of 10 top-grossing movies this year. The data table containing a series of tally marks allows you to quickly look at the marks and see who is ahead.

How Do I Make One?

All data tables have the following components:

    A. **Title.** This describes the information that is being entered into the data table. Without the descriptive title, it is entirely possible that readers might not even know what it is that they are looking at.

    For our three examples above, we could have used the following descriptive titles:
      i. Favorite Fruit in Room 4
      ii. Penny Toss, Heads or Tails?
      iii. Our Favorite Movies

    B. **Variables.** This is a word that describes the data that is being collected and the choices or options that are presented.

    C. **Boxes.** If you are going to herd sheep, you need a corral. In science, we herd and organize data within vertical and horizontal lines that form boxes and keep the data where it should be.

Heads or Tails

Penny Spin, Heads or Tails

Heads	
Tails	

Penny Flip, Heads or Tails

Heads	
Tails	

How Come, Huh?

If you examine the penny carefully, you will notice that the side that shows Lincoln's head sticks out a little and has just a bit more metal on it than the other side. This extra mass on one side has an effect on a rotating object. It creates a force called torque.

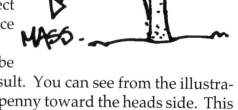

This torque, mild as it may be in this situation, affects the end result. You can see from the illustration shown here that it pushes the penny toward the heads side. This is something that should be supported by your data.

When you flip the penny into the air, the difference in mass becomes negligible and has little to no effect. Now, it simply becomes a matter of chance. Mathematical probability tells us that, if left up to chance, the penny will come up heads half the time and tails the other half. Is this what happened when you experimented? Review your data table to check.

More Data Table Basics

What Do Data Tables Look Like?

We already talked a little about the main components in a data table. However, you should also know that a complete data table has the following six characteristics:

    A. A descriptive title.
    B. A constant (uniform standard of measure).
    C. A variable describing what information is to be collected during the experiment.
    D. Units identifying how the variable and constant were measured.
    E. Data that has been collected in ordered pairs.
    F. All data herded into neat, little boxes.

Here is an example of a completed data table measuring the temperature of water while it heats to boiling:

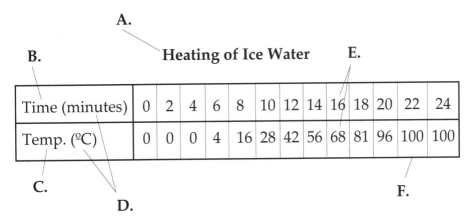

What Do They Tell Me?
A. The Title

The title, Heating of Ice Water, pretty much lays it on the line. The lab is about the heating of water that is probably pretty cold at the beginning of the lab. A good title takes all of the guesswork out of identifying what the data in the data table describes.

Data Table Basics

B. The Constant

When you look at the data table, you see two sets of data, time and temperature. If you look more carefully at the numbers, you will notice that the time readings are very consistent, every two minutes to be exact. The temperature readings, however, are all over the place. Time is called the constant in this case. It is very predictable, it is consistent, it is even. It is the base that we use to let us know when to take the temperature readings. It tells us when to collect the data on the variable being tested.

C. The Variable

The temperature readings in this example are called the variable. The reason for this is that you have no idea what the readings will be until you take them. Unlike the time, which will have advanced two minutes each time you take a reading, the temperature is irregular. Sometimes it does not change at all and sometimes there are huge jumps in temperature. It varies.

Typically, in an experiment, the variable is the thing that you are testing. It is what you want to know. How does the temperature increase, how many swings will the pendulum make, what is the average rainfall? Those are variables.

D. Units

You will notice that behind the time constant is the word minutes in parentheses. Behind the temperature reading is (°C) for Celsius. These are the units of measure for the variable and constant. They tell you how the time and temperature are going to be measured—in minutes, seconds, or hours, (or) in Celsius, Fahrenheit, or Kelvin. Without the units, you do not know how the variable and constant were measured, and the data is worthless to you.

E. Ordered Pairs

Take a peek at the data table and you will also notice that there are pairs of corresponding numbers. At 16 minutes, the temperature was 68° Celsius. Those two numbers, taken together, are called an ordered pair. Every set of numbers in a data table is an ordered pair. These pairs are really easy to pick out because they are either side by side or one atop the other.

F. Boxes

Gotta keep the sheep in the pen. The boxes make the data table look neat and presentable and make it easier to follow and interpret the data and check facts.

How Do I Make One?

Pay attention, we covered that. However, for some hands-on experience, we bequeath unto you the following lab ...

Nail Magnets

The Experiment

Take an ordinary nail, wrap it with several loops of copper wire, hook a battery to it, and you have an electromagnet—a magnet that was created when electricity flowed through a wire around an iron core.

Electromagnets are the foundation for all modern-day electric motors. Cars start and run because they have an electromagnet in the motor. Most countertop kitchen appliances, home repair tools, and other electrical devices that run with motors are powered with electromagnets.

Materials

1   Coil of bell wire
1   Pair of wire strippers/cutters
1   16-penny Nail, ungalvanized
1   Box of paper clips, small
1   Battery holder
1   D Battery
2   Alligator clips
1   Sheet of paper

Procedure

1. Cut a 24-inch length of bell wire from the coil and strip both ends. To strip the end of a wire, you place about 1/2-inch of wire into the wire stripper, clamp down, and pull the wire through the little hole. The wire stripper should cut through the plastic but not the metal, and when you pull, the plastic insulation should come off, exposing the copper wire inside.

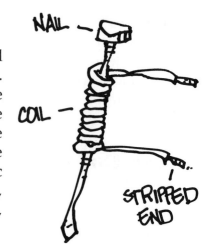

2. Leave a 4-inch tail and wrap one coil of wire around the nail as tightly as you can. Add a second coil right next to the first. Do this until you have a total of 10 coils on the nail. Use the illustration on the previous page as a guide.

Lower the nail into a pile of paper clips and see how many you can attract. Ideally none, but in the spirit of establishing a control, we had to try.

3. Snap the D battery into the battery clip and attach an alligator clip to each end of the battery clip.

4. Attach the loose end of each alligator clip to the bell wire that you stripped to complete the circuit. As soon as the circuit is complete, the electricity will start to flow through the wires wrapped around the nail—and you will have created an electromagnet.

Nail Magnets

5. Dip the electromagnet into a pile of paper clips and see how many you can pick up with your newly constructed electromagnet. Count them and record this number in the data table on this page in the box that correlates with 10 wraps.

6. Continue to experiment by increasing the number of wraps around the nail in increments of 10. Record the number of paper clips that you pick up each time.

Data & Observations

Using the data that you collected, complete the data table below. Come up with your own title. The units for the electromagnet are coil wraps, the weight is paper clips, and we already have the boxes drawn in for you.

	10	20	30	40	50

How Come, Huh?

We know that when electricity flows through a wire, it produces a magnetic field around the wire. This is because electricity is made up of electrons that are zipping through the wire, like water moving through a hose. As the electrons flow through the wire, they are lined up in an orderly fashion, producing a magnetic field that organizes the iron particles in the nail. Once the iron particles in the nail are lined up, this creates the magnetic field. The more wraps there are around the nail, the stronger the magnetic field will be.

Extended Data Tables

What Do They Look Like?

Extended data tables make more information available to the reader. They show more than just the constant and variable readings. They can be adapted and extended several ways, including the following:

    A. Addition of multiple samples. Let's say you are experimenting with plants and how they respond to filtered sunlight. Rather than bank all of your data on a single plant, you decide that it would be prudent to grow and test 10 plants, all under the same conditions, and average your results.

    In this case, your variables (plant growth) would be listed under the constant as a series of 10 horizontal rows. Each plant would have its own row. *Do the lab, Pendulum Puzzles.*

    B. Additional columns to calculate data. A lot of times, especially with physics labs, additional columns can be added to the data table, and the amount of force applied, the speed, acceleration, or other pieces of information can be calculated right in the data table. *Do the lab, Calculated Leverage.*

What Do They Tell Me?

Extended data tables allow you to 1) compare multiple samples under the same conditions and 2) calculate information in the data table, making it easy to double check your work.

How Do I Make One?

Follow the basic guidelines and simply add more columns where it is appropriate.

Pendulum Puzzles

The Experiment

You have a pendulum made out of string, a paper clip, and a couple of washers. The pendulum works just fine, but you want it to swing a little bit faster. Do you add more weight to your pendulum, lengthen the string, shorten the string, or pull the pendulum back farther so that it has more energy? Answers, please. We are all breathless in anticipation.

Materials

1   String, 90 cm long
1   Metric meterstick
1   Paper clip
3   Washers, 1.5-inch diameter
1   Hand
    Gravity

Procedure

1. Now we are going to study pendulums. There are two things that actually may affect how long it takes a pendulum to swing back and forth—the length of the pendulum and the weight of the pendulum. We are going to experiment with both. First we need to have a few rules:

    a. You will always time the swings for 30 seconds.

    b. You will always release the pendulum from the same place. Don't release it farther back one time and closer another.

    c. You will count once each time the pendulum passes your belly button.

2. To make your pendulum, you will need to bend the paper clip out into an "S" shape. Tie one end onto the string and add washers to the other end. Use the illustration shown here as a guide.

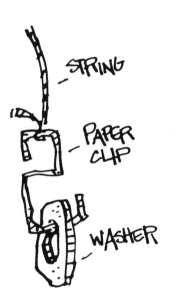

3. With the assistance of your teacher or parents, fill in the chart on the next page. To get you started, the first experiment is like this. You will put one washer on the paper clip and hold the string at a height of 30 cm. Let it swing for 30 seconds and record the number of swings in the box under 1 and next to 30 cm.

4. Now add a second washer and count for another 30 seconds; record your answer under 2 washers in the 30 cm row.

5. Finally, add a third washer and repeat the procedure.

6. Repeat this experimental sequence using a pendulum that is 45 cm, 60 cm, 75 cm, and 90 cm long. Record your data in the space provided on the next page.

Data Table Construction

This kind of data table allows you to invoke the multiple variable clause into your contract. We are going to use the title, Counting Pendulum Swings—simple, to the point, and lets readers know what they are looking at. The constant in this lab is the mass (measured in number of washers), and the variable is the length of the string (measured in centimeters). You will collect the ordered pairs and, at this point in your education, you should be able to draw a straight line with the assistance of a ruler. Time to build the data table …

Pendulum Puzzles

Counting Pendulum Swings

Mass (# Washers)	1	2	3
String # 1 (30 cm)			
String # 2 (45 cm)			
String # 3 (60 cm)			
String # 4 (75 cm)			
String # 5 (90 cm)			

How Come, Huh?

As you should be able to see from your data, the only thing that really matters in this experiment is the length of the string. The mass and the distance that you pull the string back have no effect on the speed at which the pendulum swings.

Imagine riding your bike down a hill, into a dip, and back up again. If the dip is little (short string), your trip is very quick. If the dip is large (long string), your trip is going to take a while. The mass of the washer and the amount of potential energy has no influence.

In terms of kinetic and potential energy, the pendulum gets its initial energy from your hand and stores that energy at the top of the swing. As the pendulum swings, it uses the stored energy to move on the way down. Once it passes the center point, it starts to store energy again until it gets to a point where it stops. At this point, it is full of potential energy. Gravity starts to pull on it, and kinetic energy kicks in again.

Calculated Leverage

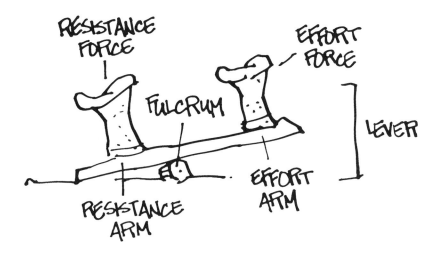

The Experiment

You should know the parts of the lever before you tackle this lab activity. To calculate the mechanical advantage of any lever, you simply have to take two measurements, the length of the effort arm and the length of the resistance arm. Divide the first length by the second. The higher the IMA, or the <u>I</u>deal <u>M</u>echanical <u>A</u>dvantage, the easier it will be to lift the object with the lever. Lab time!

Materials

- 2 Wax cups, 5 oz. each
- 1 Roll of masking tape
- 1 Ruler, 30 cm
- 1 Pencil
- 1 Box of paper clips
- 1 Rock, large, 3-inch diameter

Procedure

1. Place a loop of tape, sticky side out, on the bottom of each wax cup. Then attach the cups to the opposite ends of the ruler, as pictured on the next page.

Calculated Leverage

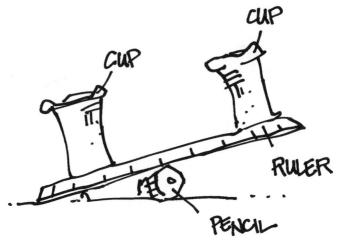

2. Place the pencil under the ruler at the 5-cm mark. The pencil should be perpendicular to the ruler, forming a funny looking plus sign when you look at the whole contraption from the top.

3. Place the rock in the cup at the 0 cm end of the ruler. Add paper clips until the rock lifts off the tabletop. Record the number of paper clips, measure the length of the effort arm and resistance arm, and calculate the IMA.

Data Table Construction

Now comes the fun part. You will need a title, and we will leave that up to you. You will also need a constant (with unit) and variable (with unit) so that this information makes sense to anyone who reads it. May we suggest the following:

       Constant: Fulcrum Location (cm)
       Variable: Effort Force (paper clips)

You will have to collect the data as ordered pairs. The box thing should be a no-brainer by now. All that is left is for you to put everything together into a concise package that we will then expand in a page or two.

Fulcrum Location (cm)	Effort Force (paper clips)
5 cm	
10 cm	
15 cm	
20 cm	
25 cm	

How Come, Huh?

IMA stands for <u>I</u>deal <u>M</u>echanical <u>A</u>dvantage. The point of using a simple machine is to give you an advantage when you are doing work. The machine takes the force that you apply to it and multiplies that force to make doing the task easier. In this case with levers, L_e stands for the length of the effort arm. This is how long the lever measures from the fulcrum to the force. L_r stands for the length of the resistance arm. That's the part that is left over. Here's the formula:

$$IMA = L_e / L_r$$

To calculate the IMA for each test, all you have to do is plug in the numbers:

IMA (15 cm fulcrum) = 15 cm / 15 cm
IMA (1 block) = 1

Calculated Leverage

The larger the IMA number, the more the machine multiplies the force that you apply to it and the easier it is to lift the rock. This is supported by the number of paper clips that needed to be added to the second cup to lift the rock. The higher the IMA, the fewer paper clips you'll need. It is a direct correlation.

To make this whole process easier, you can expand your data table to include this information also. The L_e, L_r, and *IMA* can all be added in additional columns so that you can multiply the numbers right at the spots where they are collected. Here's what it looks like when you do that ...

Data Table Construction Expanded

Complete the data table below. Be sure to add a title, enter the data you collected and calculate the values for the three right-hand columns.

Fulcrum Location (cm)	Effort Force (paper clips)	L_e	L_r	IMA
5 cm		5 cm		
10 cm			20 cm	
15 cm				1
20 cm		20 cm		
25 cm				

Big Idea 3

Once the data has been organized and recorded into a data table, a picture of that data can be constructed using pictographs, pie graphs, bar graphs, line graphs, or best fit graphs.

Graphing Basics

What Are the Parts of a Graph?

Axes (lines)
There are actually two lines—nothing fancy, no wiggles, no abstract, counterintuitive, neo–Scibbilian extracts. Just two straight lines, one going across the bottom of the page and another going up the side of the page.

A. The Horizontal Axis. This is the line that zips across the bottom of the page. It is one of the anchors for a good graph. If you have a tough time remembering which way horizontal goes, just shorten the word to horizon. Horizons are relatively level and run from left to right, separating the sky from the land.

B. The Vertical Axis. This is the line that zips up the left-hand side of the page. It is the other anchor for the graph.

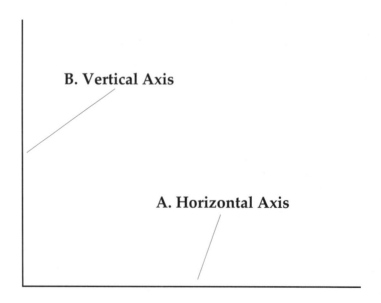

Line ID

OK, so you have these two lines. Big deal, what do they mean? Each line has a purpose. The bottom line is the home for the constant, and the vertical line is the home for the variable.

A. Constant. Just like the name suggests, this is the thing that you measure with regularity. It is predictable, it is measured at even intervals, and it forms the foundation for the experiment. Constants are things such as measuring the time every minute or increasing the weight by ten grams each trial. Constants are known going into the experiment and can be entered into data tables before the lab begins.

B. Variable. This is the thing that you are measuring. It changes, it is unpredictable, it is what you want to know about the experiment. Some examples of variables are how does the temperature change, does the speed increase, and what happens to the brightness of the bulb?

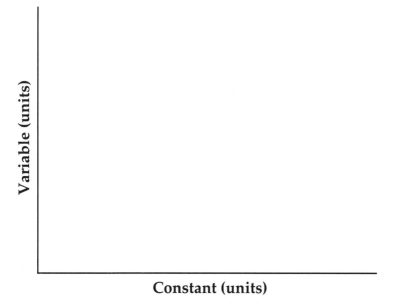

Graphing Basics

More Line ID

Things are looking up. You have two lines. You know that the horizontal axis is your constant and the vertical axis is your variable. Unfortunately, we are still missing a bit of information.

A. Units. How do you plan to measure the constant and variable—degrees Celsius, minutes, millimeters, pints, or what? What do those numbers mean along those axes? Both the constant and the variable need to be accompanied by the units that they are measured in. Without this information, the data is worthless.

B. Numerical Increments. This is a fancy term that means that you need to add numbers to identify the lines in the graph. *The numbers that you use will be determined by the constant and the data that you collect.*

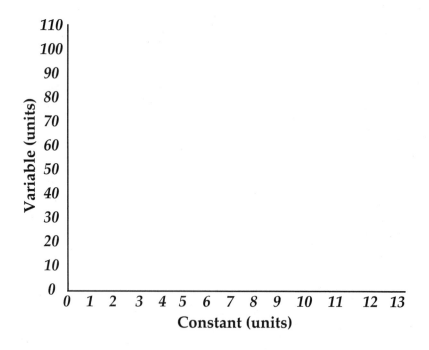

The Guts
Your graph is set up. Now all you have to do is take the data in the data table and make a picture from it. That is exactly what a graph is—a picture of the data in the data table.

A. Ordered Pairs. The data is usually collected in ordered pairs. For example, if you were heating water, your data table may read that at ten minutes (the constant), the temperature of the water might be 64º Celsius (the variable).

Find the 10-minute mark on the horizontal axis and trace an imaginary line straight up. Find the 64º line on the vertical axis and trace an imaginary line straight across. Where the two lines intersect is the data point for that ordered pair. You have just plotted a piece of the picture.

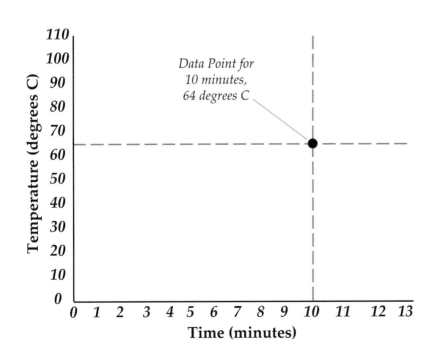

Graphing Basics

B. Data Points. You don't stop with a single set of ordered pairs. You have an entire picture to draw, so you need to enter all of the ordered pairs that you collected onto the graph as data points. When you are finished, your work could look something like this if you are heating water.

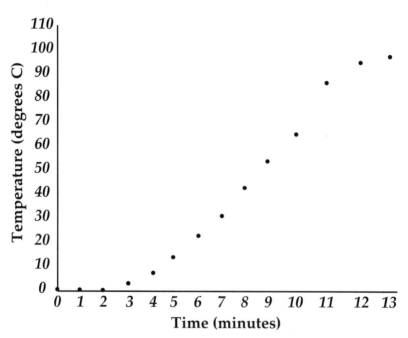

C. Bars or Lines. Once you have all of your data points plotted, then it is time for you to add bars if this is a bar graph, or lines if this is a line or a best fit graph. We are going to assume, for this example, that you are interested in presenting your data as a line graph. Once you get all of the ordered pairs plotted as data points onto the graph, nab your ruler, sharpen your pencil, and play dot-to-dot. The almost-finished product will look something like this ...

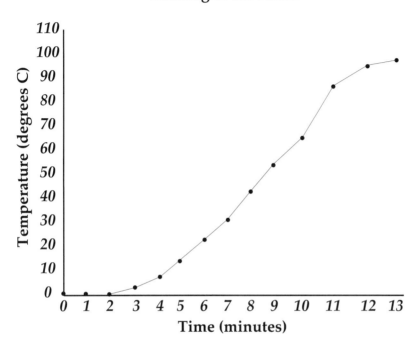

The Title

The finishing touch is the title, which tells just exactly what it is that all these numbers and lines mean. Don't be too clever or fancy; this is one place where you don't get points for being creative. The title, Heating of Ice Water, is quick, concise, and to-the-point. Thermal Accounting of Molecular Phase Changes in Simple Solvents sure sounds impressive, but unless you are a finalist in a competition for "Synaptic Whiz of the Year," it is a bit excessive. No need to trip over your shoelaces on the way out the door to recess.

So, that's it. Draw a couple of lines. Add numbers, variables, units, and a pile of dots. Throw in a line or two and give the thing a title. That is all there is to graphing.

Displaying the Data

What Do Graphs Look Like?
There are basically five kinds of graphs.

A. Pictographs. These are stacks of pictures that represent a number of objects or responses.

For example, if you were graphing the population growth of the United States, you might select a picture of a person to represent 10 million people. That information would be identified in a key. You would stack people up to represent the population in a given year. 150 million people in 1940? That would be 15 people stacked on top of one another. Got an extra 5 million you need to show? Add one-half of a person to the top of the stack. *Do the lab, Stacking Water.*

B. Pie Graphs. These are round, just as you would expect from a pie. All of the data is divided from a whole, which is 100%. Each category is given an appropriately sized slice of the pie, and that category is usually identified by name and percentage.

For example, 100 people are interviewed and 42 say beef is their favorite protein, 30 say they like chicken because everything else tastes just like it anyway, 12 like pork, 10 prefer seafood, 6 think lamb is best, while 2 choose to suck down slices of tofu to get their daily intake of protein. A pie graph of that survey is pictured at the right. *Do the lab, Conductivity Tester.*

C. Bar Graphs. These are pictographs without the pictures. They take less time, not to mention a slightly depleted imagination. Regardless, these graphs are valuable for quick reference and easy comparison. *Do the lab, Liquid Densities.*

D. Line Graphs. These are the most common kinds of graphs that you will make, see, and use. The constant is plotted along the bottom of the graph using the horizontal axis, and the variable is plotted along the left side of the graph using the vertical axis. Each ordered pair is then plotted and placed on the graph. When all of the ordered pairs have been identified, a ruler is used to connect the dots and represent the data. *Do the lab, Instant Hand Warmer.*

E. Best Fit Graphs. These are used to make predictions, find averages, and graph tendencies. Everything about the best fit graph is identical to the line graph, except that when it comes time to connect the dots, you don't. Instead, you look at all of the dots and draw a freehand line through the bulk of the dots, following the tendency but not necessarily connecting one dot to another. This type of graph is great when you need to take averages, see trends, and make educated guesses. *Do the lab, Heli Data.*

Stacking Water

The Experiment

This lab will allow you to review how to use tabulation data tables with an extended twist, as well as how to collect data to be plotted on a pictograph.

To do this lab, you will start with your drinking glass completely full of water. We define "completely full" as the water level being exactly even with the top of the container. You are then going to add small paper clips, one at a time, until the water just dribbles over the edge of the rim.

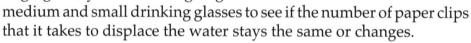

Once you collect the data for the large glass, you are then going to fill medium and small drinking glasses to see if the number of paper clips that it takes to displace the water stays the same or changes.

Materials

1   Large drinking glass
1   Medium drinking glass
1   Small drinking glass
2   Boxes of 100 small paper clips
    Water

Procedure

1. Fill the large drinking glass so that the water is perfectly level across the very top.

2. Start adding and counting paper clips. Don't stop until you finally add one clip too many and the water in your glass spills over onto the table. In the data table on the next page, record the number of paper clips that you added to achieve this glorious feat.

3. Repeat this procedure, adding, counting, recording, and eventually spilling the water out of the different sized glasses and onto the table. In the end, you will have completed your data table below.

Tabulation Data Table
Adding Paper Clips to Drinking Glasses

	# Paper Clips Added
Glass #1	
Glass #2	
Glass #3	

How Come, Huh?

Every time you add a paper clip to the glass, the paper clip sinks to the bottom of your container. As it does this, it pushes up a tiny bit of water exactly equal to its volume. After a couple of paper clips, you would normally think that this would cause a very full container to spill some of the liquid out of the glass and onto the table. But because water molecules are attracted to each other—a phenomenon called cohesion—they hang onto their buddies if it looks like one of them might fall over the edge.

Stacking Water

If you could see a water molecule, it would look like Mickey Mouse's head. The oxygen atom has a negative charge, and the two hydrogen atoms have a positive charge. The result is a molecule that acts like a magnet.

As more and more paper clips are added to the drinking glass, more and more water molecules are shoved up out of the container and appear to be balancing above the rim. What is actually happening is the water molecules are attracted to one another and are not easily pulled apart. To avoid being displaced, they form a bulge—visual evidence of surface tension.

This goes on for a while, the bulge growing with every paper clip that is added. Eventually gravity takes its toll on the water molecules, they cannot hang on to one another any longer, and some of them dribble over the edge. If you watch carefully, they go as a group, clinging to one another all the way down to the tabletop.

Data Tables to Pictographs

We have collected the data and have learned why the number of paper clips is so much greater than we thought it might be. Now it is time to create a pictograph of the data.

The pictograph is created directly from the data that is collected. The title is the same. The variables and units are identical. You plot the data using the numbers and, instead of neat boxes, you use vertical and horizontal axes to organize the data.

Creating a Pictograph

A complete pictograph has seven characteristics:

   A. A descriptive title.
   B. A constant (uniform standard of measure).
   C. A variable describing what information is to be collected during the experiment.
   D. Units identifying how the variable and constant were measured.
   E. Data that has been collected in ordered pairs.
   F. All data herded into neat, little boxes.
   G. A key that indicates the value of the picture.

Using the information in this lab, fill in the blanks:

   Title: _____
   Constant : _____
      Unit used: _____
   Variable: _____
      Unit used: _____
   Data Collected
      Glass #1 : _____ paper clips
      Glass #2 : _____ paper clips
      Glass #3 : _____ paper clips

On the next page, you'll find horizontal and vertical axes that are ready for you to use to complete a pictograph.

Stacking Water

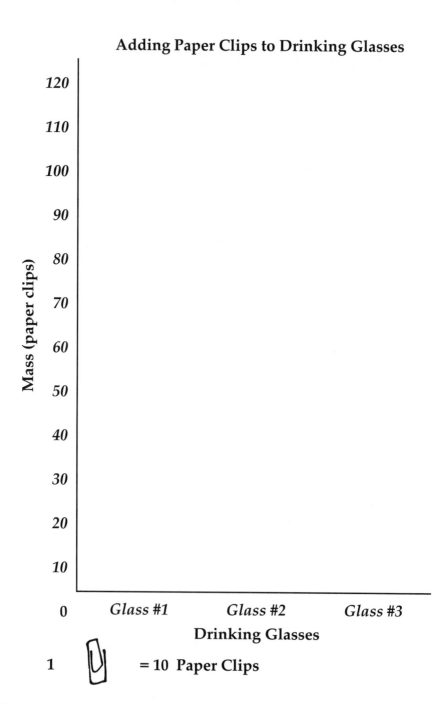

Conductivity Tester

The Experiment
Electrons are found in every atom. They are knocked loose and are bumped around all the time, but they do not have the ability to pass through all materials. In fact, they don't travel very well at all in materials called insulators. The materials that do allow electrons to zip on through are called conductors. This lab will introduce you to a technique that will allow you to test any material and determine if it is a conductor or an insulator. You will also use this experiment as an opportunity to make a new data table as well as construct a pie graph.

Materials
- 1 Battery with battery holder
- 1 Lamp with socket
- 3 Alligator clips
- 1 Nail, 8 penny
- 1 Copper wire, 18 gauge, 3 inches
- 1 Craft stick
- 1 Strip of fabric, 1 inch by 4 inches
- 1 Glass microscope slide
- 1 Plastic straw
- 1 Paper clip
- 1 Buzzer

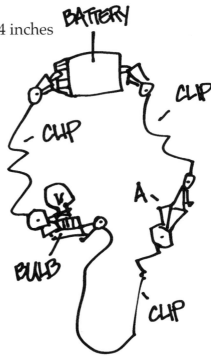

Procedure
1. Snap the battery into the battery holder. Bend out the tabs on the ends of the clip so the alligator clips can be attached easily.

2. Assemble the circuit pictured at the right and make sure that the bulb lights up when everything is connected together.

Conductivity Tester

3. Separate the two alligator clips (point A in the circuit) and test the nail by clipping it between the two alligator clips that you just separated. If the light goes on, that particular item is a conductor; if it remains unlit, it is an insulator.

4. Test each of the items in the data table one at a time by clipping them into the circuit. Mark the appropriate box in the data table below for each test.

Data & Observations

Mark whether each is an insulator or a conductor:

Item	Conductor	Insulator
Nail		
Copper Wire		
Craft Stick		
Buzzer		
Fabric		
Microscope Slide		
Plastic Straw		
Lamp with Socket		
Alligator Clip		
Paper Clip		

How Come, Huh?

What you should have discovered is that metal objects make excellent conductors, while objects made of wood, glass, plastic, fabric, and other kinds of materials do not.

The main difference between these two is that the metals have a very orderly, simple, crystalline structure, whereas the others have more complex arrangements of molecules. The simplicity of the design for metals allows the electrons to flow freely through them, passing from atom to atom.

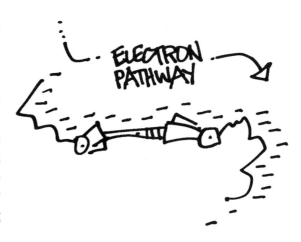

Creating a Pie Graph

A complete pie graph has three characteristics:

    A. A descriptive title.
    B. A big circle divided into percentage pieces.
    C. Data, as pie pieces, identified.

Using the information in this lab, fill in the blanks:

    A. Title: _____

    B. Data Collected

        # of conductors _____ %

        # of insulators _____ %

Conductivity Tester

Here is an example of a pie graph that is set up and ready for you to fill in for this experiment. Of the 10 samples that you tested, determine what percentage of insulators and conductors were in the sample. Then divide the circle below accordingly.

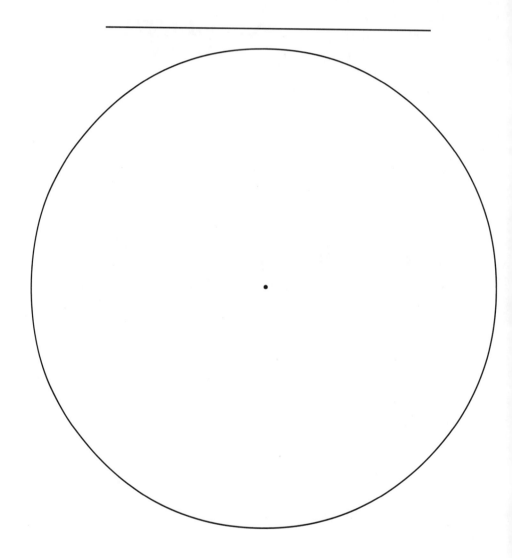

Liquid Densities

The Challenge

Density is a word that describes how tightly packed the atoms inside a material are. For example, if you were to take two rocks, pumice and granite, you would find that they are made out of exactly the same mix of minerals. They are identical, except that the granite was formed when a big blob of molten rock cooled very slowly underground, and the pumice was formed when the exact same molten mass of rock was spit out of a volcano. If you placed both rocks in water, the granite would sink and the pumice would float. The granite is denser than, or packed tighter together than, the pumice.

Another way to explore this idea is using liquids. All liquids have different densities. If you could shrink down to the size of an atom and could swim around inside a glass of water and a glass of corn syrup, you could compare which one was more crowded. Chances are the corn syrup would win that contest. The lab you are about to do will allow you compare the different densities of five liquids.

Materials

1   Triple beam balance
1   50 mL Beaker
    50 mL Water
    50 mL Rubbing alcohol
    50 mL Glycerine
    50 mL Corn syrup
    50 mL Cooking oil

Liquid Densities

Procedure

1. Zero out your triple beam balance.

2. Once you are certain that your balance is calibrated, take a 50 mL beaker and place it on the scale. Weigh the beaker and enter that weight into the column on the data table that is labeled Weight of Beaker (g).

3. Add 50 mL of water to the 50 mL beaker and place it onto the scale. Determine the weight of the beaker with the water in it and enter that number into the column labeled Beaker + Liquid (g).

4. Repeat this process with the other four liquids.

5. When you have finished weighing the five liquids, determine the net weight of each liquid by subtracting the weight of the empty beaker from the weight of the beaker with the liquid in it:

> Gross Weight   Beaker with liquid
>   – <u>Beaker empty</u>
> Net Weight   Weight of liquid

6. Calculate the density of each liquid using the formula, density = mass/volume. You just calculated the mass of each liquid sample in Step 5 and you know that you used 50 mL of liquid each time. The quick way to do this is ...

> Density of Liquid = Mass of Liquid / 50 mL

Data Table

Fill in each of the columns in this data table as you complete the steps in the experiment.

Relative Densities of Common Liquids

Liquid (50 mL)	Weight of Beaker (g)	Beaker + Liquid (g)	Net Weight (g)	Density (g/mL)
Water				
Corn Syrup				
Alcohol				
Glycerine				
Cooking Oil				

Creating a Bar Graph

A complete bar graph has six characteristics:

    A. A descriptive title.
    B. A constant (uniform standard of measure).
    C. A variable describing what information is to be collected during the experiment.
    D. Units identifying how the variable and constant were measured.
    E. Data that has been collected in ordered pairs.
    F. All data herded into neat, little boxes.

Liquid Densities

Creating a Bar Graph

Using the information in this lab, fill in the blanks:

Title: _____

Constant: <u>Type of Liquid</u>

Variable: _____

    Unit used: <u>grams</u>

Data Collected

    Density of Water: <u>1.0</u> g/mL

    Density of Corn Syrup: _____ g/mL

    Density of Alcohol: _____ g/mL

    Density of Glycerine: _____ g/mL

    Density of Cooking Oil: _____ g/mL

To plot the density of water, you create a bar that starts just above the word Water and extends to the 1.0 g/mL mark. Bars in a bar graph are usually solid.

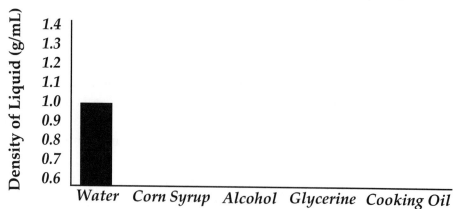

Using the data that you collected in the experiment, complete the bar graph.

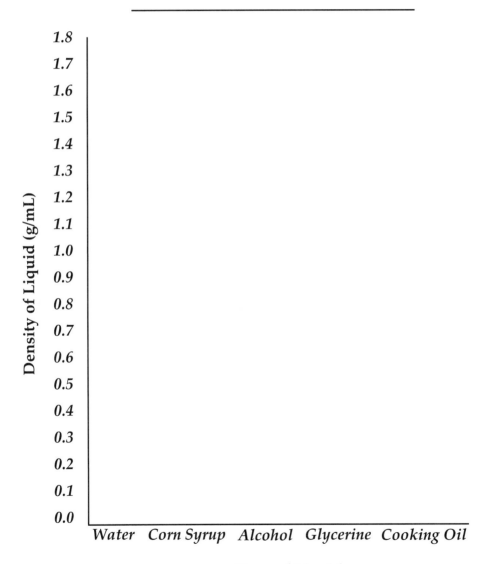

Instant Hand Warmer

The Experiment
Two chemicals will be mixed in a sealed container. When the gas pressure increases to the point where the container fails, we will have a small and very polite explosion of gas.

Materials
1   Beaker, 250 mL
1   Thermometer, °C/°F
1   Calcium chloride, 1 oz.
1   Resealable baggie
    Water

Procedure

1. Using the beaker, measure out 150 mL of warm water. Add that 150 mL of water to the baggie. If you don't have a measuring cup, fill the bag until there is about an inch of water in it. **(Be sure to use warm water. Using cold water will change the experiment significantly.)**

2. Place the thermometer in the water and take an initial reading. Enter that number into the data table on the next page.

3. Remove the cap from the calcium chloride bottle and add four caps of calcium chloride to the water. Insert the thermometer and zip the baggie closed. As the chemical starts to dissolve, you should notice a significant increase in temperature.

4. Record the temperature every minute for 10 minutes.

Data Table

Fill in each of the columns in this data table as you complete the steps in the experiment.

Heating of Water with Calcium Chloride

Time (min.)										
Temp. (°C)										

Creating a Line Graph

A complete line graph has six characteristics:

A. A descriptive title.
B. A constant (uniform standard of measure).
C. A variable describing what information is to be collected during the experiment.
D. Units identifying how the variable and constant were measured.
E. Data that has been collected in ordered pairs.
F. All data herded into neat, little boxes.

Instant Hand Warmer

Creating a Line Graph

Using the information in this lab, fill in the blanks:

Title: _____

Constant : _____

    Unit used: _____

Variable: _____

    Unit used: _____

Data Collected: Ordered pairs

To plot the temperature change in water, you look at the ordered pairs.

    A. Start with the first constant, time at 0 minutes, and draw an imaginary line straight up from that point on the horizontal axis.

    B. Next find the first variable, temperature (ºC), that is matched with time at 0 minutes. Draw an imaginary line straight across from that reading.

    C. Where the lines from this ordered pair intersect (cross) is the data point for that ordered pair. Put a dot in that spot.

    D. Repeat this process for all of the ordered pairs in the data table.

    E. Finally, when all of the ordered pairs have been plotted, start with the first dot and draw a straight line from it to the second dot. Then connect the second dot to the third and continue on until you have connected all of the dots and until every ordered pair has been represented.

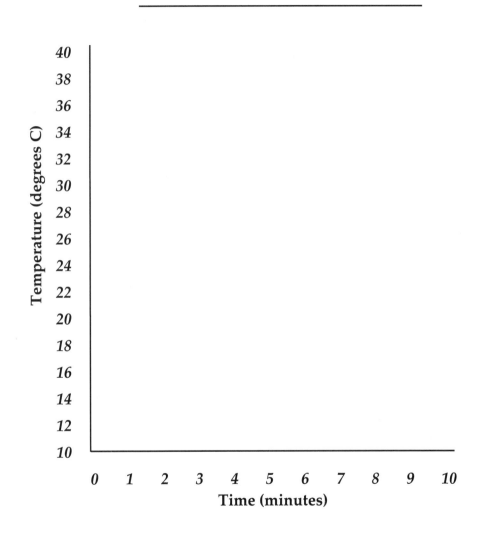

How Come, Huh?

When calcium chloride is mixed with water, it splits apart, forming calcium ions and chloride ions. When this happens, the energy that was holding those atoms together is released as heat. That is why the bag started to feel warm as the reaction proceeded.

Heli Data

The Experiment

You will cut a piece of paper and fold it into a design that twirls to the ground like a helicopter. After the initial *ooh aah*, you can then very easily take this idea and produce a myriad of variations on this basic design.

We are going to explore, record, and then plot the relationship between the surface area of the rotors (wings) and the amount of time that it takes for the helicopter to fall to the ground.

Materials

1   Pair of scissors
1   Piece of paper
1   Clock with second hand
1   Metric ruler
1   Chair
    Atmosphere

Procedure

1. Use the pattern on the next page as a template to be traced onto the piece of paper. Cut the design out along the perimeter and save the extra paper for additional projects.

2. Cut along the dashed lines. Once these cuts are made, fold one of the long strips (A) toward you, creasing it along the solid line, and the other (B) away from you. These are the rotors of the helicopter, and at this point, it should look like a giant capital I with bunny ears.

3. Once the rotors are made, fold the sides (C & D) into the middle just like you would fold a letter. This is the body of the helicopter.

4. The last thing to do is to fold the bottom (E) of the helicopter up about a half an inch. This fold helps keep everything together. A cartoon of what the final contraption should look like is shown on the page at the left.

5. Assume the helicopter flying position: Stand on the chair, extend the arm with the helicopter straight out into the air, and place your other hand on your hip. Drop said invention from outstretched arm. Make appropriate *ooh aah* noises. If the spirit of Sir Newton is with you, the helicopter will twirl to the floor.

6. Now that the excitement has subsided, drop the helicopter again and record the amount of time in seconds that it takes to hit the floor once it leaves your hands.

7. Pick the helicopter up, measure 2 cm from the tip of each rotor, and snip the paper off the rotor. In effect, you are shortening the rotor and reducing the surface area pushing against the air in the room.

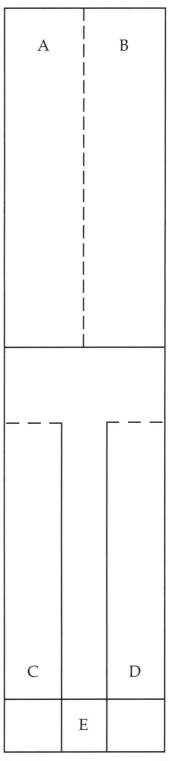

Heli Data

8. Drop the helicopter from the same exact height as in your first trial and record the amount of time that it takes for the helicopter to hit the floor. Enter your data into the data table.

9. Snip another 2 cm from the tip of each rotor so that each is 6 cm long. Drop and record the amount of time it takes for it to hit the floor. Continue to shorten the rotors by 2 cm each time and record the time that it takes to fall to the floor. These are the readings for Helicopter #1.

10. Create another helicopter that has a shorter body but with rotors still at 10 cm. Drop and record the time for this short body version. Snip 2 cm off at a time and fill in the data table. These are the readings for Helicopter #2.

11. Finally, create a third helicopter that has a longer body but with rotors still at 10 cm. Drop and record the time for this long body version. Snip 2 cm off at a time and fill in the data table. These are the readings for Helicopter #3.

Data Table

Surface Area, Mass, and Speed of Descent

Helicopter Rotors (cm)	10	8	6	4	2	0
Time #1 (sec)						
Time #2 (sec)						
Time #3 (sec)						

Creating a Best Fit Graph

A complete best fit graph has six characteristics:

A. A descriptive title.
B. A constant (uniform standard of measure).
C. A variable describing what information is to be collected during the experiment.
D. Units identifying how the variable and constant were measured.
E. Data that has been collected in ordered groups.
F. A line that is drawn freehand and extends beyond the actual numbers of the data that has been collected.

Using the information in this lab, fill in the blanks:

Title: _____

Constant : _____

     Unit used: _____

Variable: _____

     Unit used: _____

Data Collected: Ordered groups

    When you look at this data table, you can see that you have three sets of ordered pairs. Rotors and Time #1, Rotors (again) and Time #2, and Rotors (a third time) and Time #3.
    Plot all of the ordered pairs from the first two columns of data. Then, plot the ordered pairs from the first and third columns, and finally plot the data from the first and fourth columns. When you are finished, you should have data points all over the graph.

Heli Data

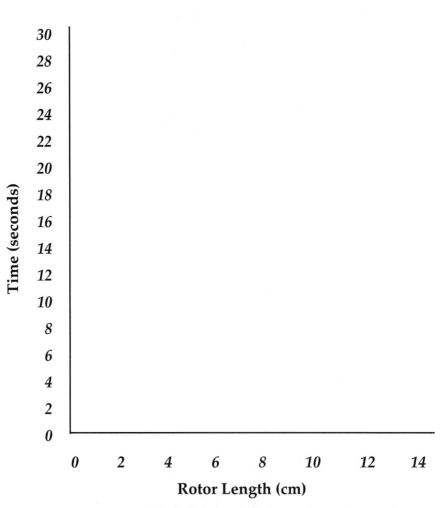

Once you get all of the sets of data plotted, you have two choices. You can make what is called a multiple line graph by connecting all of the data from the first two sets into a line, then the second two, and finally the third set. This would give you three lines. Or you can draw a single line sorta–kinda through most of the data to make a best fit graph.

How Come, Huh?

This is a simple exercise in air friction. As the helicopter falls to the floor, the air molecules push up against the blades and slow the descent. It spins because the blades are on opposite sides, causing unbalanced forces that spin the 'copter, resisting the fall, so that the rotors spin faster.

By changing the mass of the base of the helicopter, we were affecting the rate at which the helicopter fell. More mass means that it has more inertia and it is harder to turn. Likewise, the lighter the helicopter is, the more quickly it starts to spin.

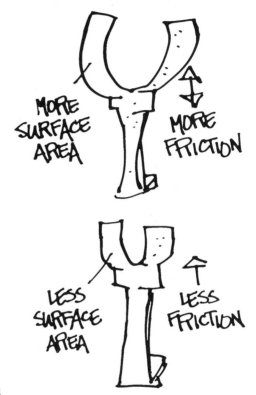

Graphs and Uses

Multiple line graphs allow you to compare three tests that are identical except for the fact that the variable has been altered.

Best fit graphs come in handy because they allow you to make predictions. You can see on the opposite page that we extended the rotor length well beyond the 10 cm that were in the instructions. By drawing in a best fit line, you are able to "predict" or guesstimate what the approximate time of descent might be if you were to actually use a helicopter with rotors that long.

Glossary

Axis, Horizontal
The line that runs along the bottom of a graph, the way the horizon line runs between sky and land. This is used to plot the constant.

Axis, Vertical
The line that runs up the side of a graph. It is used to plot the variable.

Bar Graph
A picture of data that is depicted using bars that rise directly from the horizontal axis. The height of the bar corresponds to the value of the variable being measured.

Best Fit Graph
This type of graph consists of a freely drawn line that allows the scientist to estimate values that have not been directly recorded. This type of graph starts out just like a line graph, but then a line is eyeballed through the data.

Cast
A replica, typically made of plaster of Paris, of a specimen that has been collected. An impression of the object is made using clay, and then the impression in the clay is filled in with plaster. When it hardens, you have an exact physical replica of the item.

Chemical Change
A change that occurs when two different chemicals are mixed together and light, heat, sound, an odor, a color change, or change of state occurs to produce an entirely new chemical.

Chromatography
The process of taking a solution, placing a drop of it on porous paper, and allowing a solvent to migrate up the length of the paper, separating pigments out by weight as it goes.

Glossary

Cohesion
An electromagnetic attraction of water molecules to one another. This is due to the fact that the hydrogen atoms are stacked on top of the oxygen atom in the molecule. When this happens, one side of the molecule has a net negative charge and the other side has a net positive charge, creating a mini-magnet.

Collection
Stuff that you find and group together based on a common thread. You might collect different types of leaves, rocks, minerals, fossils, or animals casts.

Conductor
An object that allows electricity to flow through it. A conductor is typically made of metal.

Constant
When you are collecting data, you should only be evaluating one thing about the experiment. This thing is called the variable, which is the thing that changes over time. A constant, on the other hand, is the part of the experiment that you know ahead of time. It changes in a very predictable manner. Time taken every minute is an example of a constant measurement. It is predictable and constant.

Crystal
A symmetrical pattern of chemicals that is visible to the naked eye. So much for romance, eh? A term used to describe an organized structure that occurs naturally in rocks and minerals or is grown in chemistry labs.

Data
Data is information. It can take the form of physical measurements, written observations, drawings, chemical changes, impressions, collections, photographs, digital images, or sound recordings.

Glossary

Data Point
A data point is produced when an ordered pair from the data table is plotted on a line or best fit graph. The data point looks like a dot. When incorporated into a graph, the dots are either connected or used as a general reference for the location of the line.

Data Table, Extended
An extended data table is a data table that not only shows the variable and constant(s) but also allows room for additional information like calculations or formulas.

Data Table, Multiple Variable
This is a data table that allows you to compare several samples undergoing the same tests. For example, if you were testing the effect of fertilizer on a particular kind of plant, and you were testing ten plants rather than a single one, a multiple variable data table would have ten columns, one for each plant, and you would be able to compare their growth very easily.

Data Table, Single Variable
A single variable data table is just that, a data table that gives you space to record a single constant and a single variable, nothing more, nothing less.

Data Table, Tabulation
A tabulation data table is used when you are collecting a large amount of data and you have one or two choices that you are soliciting from the sample.

Drawing
Pretty much what it sounds like—a picture created when someone puts a pen or pencil to a sheet of paper to draw an object.

Glossary

Electromagnet
A magnet produced when an electric current passes through a wire wrapped around an iron core. The magnetic field produced by the wire coil creates a magnetic field around the core, and the wire-wrapped core becomes a magnet itself.

Ideal Mechanical Advantage
A measure of the amount of force that a simple machine gives to the person who is using it. The higher the number, the more work the machine does for the person.

Impression
An impression is created by smooshing an object into a piece of clay to create a replica of that object.

Information
Information is data. It can take the form of physical measurements, written observations, drawings, chemical changes, impressions, collections, photographs, digital images, or sound recordings.

Lever
A lever is a simple machine that is designed to give the lifter an advantage when trying to move heavy objects. It generally consists of an effort arm rotating around a fulcrum, applying force to the resistance arm. A teeter-totter is an excellent example of a lever, as are shovels, crowbars, and tire irons.

Line Graph
A line graph is designed to create a linear picture of the data that has been collected. The ordered pairs are plotted as data points on the horizontal and vertical axes of the graph. Once the data points are plotted, a line connecting all of the dots is drawn. The end product is a line graph.

Glossary

Optical Illusion
A drawing that can fool the brain into seeing something that is not there or disguising or disorienting something that is there.

Ordered Pair
Two pieces of data, one variable and one constant, that are collected in direct relationship to each other. The constant is determined, and at the appropriate time, the variable is collected. Together, this data is called an ordered pair.

Pendulum
A suspended weight that swings freely from a fulcrum.

Pictograph
A graph that uses pictures to represents fixed quantities of a certain item. For example, one apple may represent 10 bushels of apples during a harvest season. If the farmer records sixteen and a half apples for his total harvest, he would have picked 165 bushels of apples. The pictograph provides a quick and easy way to determine a quantity of something.

Pie Graph
A pie graph is a circular graph that depicts percentages of information as pieces of a pie. There is usually no more than 100% allocated for any pie graph. The pie is sliced into appropriately sized pieces to show percentages of the whole.

Pitch
How high or low a note is when it is played on a musical instrument. The pitch of an instrument is directly influenced by the instrument's length. The higher the pitch, the shorter the instrument, and vice-versa.

Glossary

Rubbing
A picture of an object that is created by placing a piece of paper or fabric over an item and rubbing it with a crayon. The pressure of the crayon changes as the crayon is rubbed over parts of the surface, and colored wax is left behind to show a picture.

Title
A title should be written above any data table or graph. It should be short, concise, and should explain very clearly what it is that the viewer is looking at.

Unit
A unit is an increment of measure that tells how the constant and variable are measured. Units can be liters, meters, or grams, as well as degrees Celsius or Fahrenheit. Units can also express time measured in seconds, minutes, or hours. There are many other examples of units, as well. A unit tells how the constant and the variable were measured.

Variable
The item that you are testing for during an experiment. It is the one thing that you are most curious about.

Index

Axis,
    horizontal, 64
    vertical, 64

Bar graphs, 68, 71, 83–85
Best fit graphs, 71, 93–95
Boxes, 47, 51

Casts, 38–43
Chemical changes, 33
Chromatography, 33–37
Cohesion, 73
Collections, 38–43
Conductors, 77–80
Constant, 50, 65
Crystals, 30–32

Data, 15
Data points, 68
Data tables,
    extended, 55
    multiple variable, 45
    single variable, 45
    tabulation, 45, 47
Drawings, 28–29

Electromagnets, 52–54

Ideal Mecanical Advantage, 59–62
Impressions, 38–43

Lab Safety, 8–10
Levers, 59–62
Line graphs, 68–69, 71, 87–89

Index

National Content Standards, 6
Numerical increments, 66

Opinions, 21
Optical illusions, 22–27
Ordered pairs, 51, 67

Pendulums, 56–58
Physical measurements, 16–17
Pictographs, 70, 74–76
Pie graphs, 70, 77, 79–80
Pitch, 19–20

Recommended Materials Suppliers, 11
Rubbings, 39, 42

Title, 47, 49, 69

Units, 51, 66

Variable, 47, 50, 65

Notes

Notes

Notes

Notes

Notes

Notes

Notes

Notes

More Science Books

Catch a Wave
50 hands-on lab activities that sound off on the topic of noise, vibration, waves, the Doppler Effect, and associated ideas.

Thermodynamic Thrills
50 hands-on lab activities that investigate heat via conduction, convection, radiation, specific heat, and temperature.

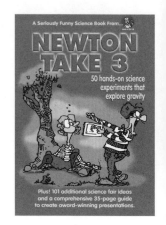

Newton Take 3
50 hands-on lab activities that explore the world of mechanics, forces, gravity, and Newton's three laws of motion.

Gravity Works
50 hands-on lab activities from the world of things that fly. Air, air pressure, Bernoulli's law, and all things that fly, float, or glide are explored.

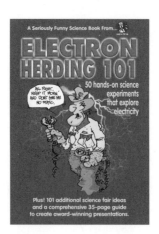

Electron Herding 101
50 hands-on lab activities that introduce static electricity, circuit electricity, and include a number of fun and very easy-to-build projects.

Opposites Attract
50 hands-on lab activities that delve into the world of natural and man-made magnets as well as the characteristics of magnetic attraction.